MY POETRY

Lewis Ernest Davies

LEWIS ERNEST DAVIES
KINGSTEIGNTON   NEWTON ABBOT   DEVON

© Lewis Ernest Davies, 2017
First published in Great Britain, 2017

The moral rights of the author have been asserted.

All rights reserved.
No part of this publication may be reproduced
or transmitted in any form or by any means,
electronic or mechanical, including photocopy,
recording, or any information storage and
retrieval system, without permission
in writing from the copyright holder.

British Library Cataloguing-in-Publication Data.
A catalogue record for this book is available
from the British Library.

ISBN 978-1-5262-0653-4
Printed in Great Britain by
Arthur H. Stockwell Ltd
Torrs Park   Ilfracombe
Devon EX34 8BA

CONTENTS

Evolution	7
It's Just Out There	7
Fluctuating	8
Trance	8
Back to College	9
Tulip Rings	10
Much Aligned, Each One Entwined	10
Bewildering Thoughts	11
Constructive	12
Inscrutable Delight	12
Master of Illusion	13
Devotion	13
Looking for a Miracle	14
Hope for Redemption	15
Water the Flowerbeds above the Ivy	15
How It Feels	16
What's Learnt	17
Tiddles Mee Squiddles Poodily Toots	17
Falling in Love	18
Corruption	19
Paved the Waves above the Seas	20
Tranquillizing Stills	20
Sheer Divine Audacity	21
Never-ending Wars	21
Winter's Fire	22
Diverging Through the Decadence	22
Freedoms	23
Incandescent With Rage	23
An Illustrious Hedgehog	24
The Answer to It All	25
Superstitious	25
Forever in a Bubble	26

Sanctity's Amiss	26
Isolation	27
Feelings	28
Extolling the Reverence	29
Encouragement	29
Senseless Conclusions	30
If the Good Come Together	32
Disingenuous	33
A Fortuitous Mess	33
Waiting	34
Sky	35
Love	35
Alternate Reality	36
There's No Restart	36
Moving on	37
Cold	38
Manipulation	39
Hey, Darling	39
No Need for Hate	40
What Happened to Those Times of Romance?	40
Conspicuous Sounds	41
Attraction	41
Anti-Bullies	42
Casuistry at Light	42
Tireless Emotion	43
Prophetic Profusion	43
Emotionally Detached	43
Multifarious Conjectures	44
Stature	45
Apathy	45
Lack of Thought	46
Rainclouds	46
No Point in Debating	47
Spiritual	47

Reclusion	48
Severing My Soul	48
Shining Sun	49
Solace	50
Mass Pollution	50
Floating	51
Falling	51
Act Like I Mean Nothing	52
Bridled with Joy	53
Stigma	53
Shallow World	54
Bland	54
Stultifying	55
Dying Dreams	55
No Appreciation	55
Accusations	56
Contradictions	56
Ambitions	57
Nepotism	57
Encumbering	58
Sunshine on the Horizon	58
Salubrious	59
Bring Me Elation	59
Uninspiring	60
Encourage and Support	60
Substance	61
Serenading Hopeless Treasures	61
In Need of Fun	62
Rhythmless Passion	62
Work	63
Despotism	64

EVOLUTION

Waiting for evolution, dusting off the prints,
eternal scepticism,
won't make me move an inch.

IT'S JUST OUT THERE

It's not as bad as it seems
people still living despite broken dreams
it's different in the city
there's much more smiling, much less pity
it's mostly online where you witness the hate
they try to end hope but it's never too late
give it a break, the technological life
it only causes doubt, only causes strife
appreciate the beauty we're all lucky to see
the beautiful sky, birds singing in trees
I can't put you at ease, tell you it'll all be fine
but appreciating nature is a better way to spend time.

FLUCTUATING

Fluctuating through the senses,
of imaginary fail
succinct illuminations,
without a countess to its tail
falling on the virtues, of subsidies divide
in amongst the wrath,
there stands a wounded pride.

TRANCE

Romance that trance when it starts to advance
if you want to play chess, then I'll do a dance.

BACK TO COLLEGE

Another train journey
no progression
life's gone by
haven't learned my lesson
summon up the energy
to get off
with my feet low down
and my head aloft
walk up to college
it's like time hasn't passed
the same old buildings
on the same old grass
go inside
nowhere to hide
silly little giggles
from soon-to-be brides
everyone's a clone
repeated conversation
talk about boredom
and indignation
the start of class
I sit alone
until some girl turns my heart to stone
you see, it wasn't a sight
for sore eyes
her amorous look
caught me by surprise.

TULIP RINGS

Don't know about coffee tables and tulip rings
but I'm listening to Vandross and he likes to sing.

MUCH ALIGNED, EACH ONE ENTWINED

Much aligned, each one entwined
renaissance asperity is due
refulgent you are,
cognizance afar
hereditary, solemnly blue.

BEWILDERING THOUGHTS

Bewildering thoughts on these stainless premises
encountering noughts like you're my arch-nemesis
pain can't be bought
or your goal to cherish it
I seek love
and aim to replenish wit
Inspiring the dissident imperial vogues
I have now laid a mile of hedgerows
all flourished and puerile
upon waves of seduction
there lies an emperor
who toils with destruction.

CONSTRUCTIVE

It's been constructive, quite productive,
a little seductive, I am spare
but then the people come back
and it's all hit the sack
and there's nothing left to prepare.

INSCRUTABLE DELIGHT

Inscrutable delight at a meeting
which felt so right
equanimity out of sight
now they've gone, so has the light.

MASTER OF ILLUSION

The master of illusion
an ambassador of perfusion
I even hold the key to the gates of confusion
but in all seriousness, I'm not a fan of drugs,
I'm not a fan of violence
I like to promote morals, not be a tool of compliance.

DEVOTION

There's no potion in the lotion
without your devotion
if you're sinking without a current
you're not in the ocean.

LOOKING FOR A MIRACLE

From the four corners of the Earth
I've got to mind my turf
I've got to have a mission
to exist is not enough
I'm looking for a miracle
I'm searching for a star
not sure how much more I can give,
now I've come this far
in retreat against resistance
I ain't got no family plan
not talking to thy neighbour
has got me where I am.

HOPE FOR REDEMPTION

Accountability is prevalent but in society
becomes irrelevant
no such hope for redemption
in our pain comes neglection.

WATER THE FLOWERBEDS ABOVE THE IVY

Wake up, have a coffee
water the flowerbeds above the ivy
tickle the leaves before sunrise
pickle on the sandwiches, dent the prize.

HOW IT FEELS

Soothing voice, smooth skin
pigmented channels, wearing thin
is it a sin, that I love you this much
devouring your breath, like it's our
last touch?
I'm convulsing now, into a heap on the floor
foraging through rainclouds, swept in from shore
I shall worry no more, fermenting eyesore
releasing this harness,
it's you I adore.

WHAT'S LEARNT

What's learnt? What's relevant?
How did it apply?
What's gone is sacrosanct
just give it another try.

TIDDLES MEE SQUIDDLES POODILY TOOTS

Tiddles Mee Squiddles likes to talk in riddles
I dreamt of her presence but it's never-ending giggles.

FALLING IN LOVE

OK dear,
I see, I see
for we're riding free,
so late at night, less oxygen
to my brain is giving my mind a fright
such delight, such delight
this is proving to be
not quite there, full of uncertainty
for I love you, you see
such happiness upon me
not nocturnal, nor bright
nor fluorescent or true
but butterscotch will melt
and will melt upon you.

CORRUPTION

Corrupt governments aplenty
controlling our every move
sucking us dry of our emotion
why doesn't life just run smooth?
But we just sit back and take it
waiting for the dust to subside
well it's never going to happen
so make a stand for your pride
heading for the great unknown
if we don't act now, no excuse to moan
take more from the rich, give more to the poor
don't allow tax breaks, enforce the law
less wastage to Europe
hand the public more control
provide jobs for the young to help us out this hole
less selfish acts of greed
more shared wealth
a complete reconstruction,
with altruists at the helm.

PAVED THE WAVES ABOVE THE SEAS

I've paved the waves above the seas,
drowning minnows, drowning fleas
for one halfpenny, the penny must drop
I'm not the one who made the mouse pop.

TRANQUILLIZING STILLS

A sense of calmness reverberating around the chills
of a midsummer night
tranquillizing stills of mixed proportions
diminishing in their might
accentuating the gills are some magic pills making
all seem all right
but as nostalgia starts to drill
there's no more time to fill
and a happy ending appears out of sight.

SHEER DIVINE AUDACITY

Walking by, pretending to not see
sheer divine audacity
lucrative but suppressed, a seraphic encore
a relationship's inception, of that I am sure.

NEVER-ENDING WARS

Wars all around the world
irrational reasons, acts absurd
innocent civilians losing their lives
no sign of hope,
no compromise
so many sad faces, so sad to see
when was heart replaced with such brutality?
Is there any glint of light in these
gaping divides?
I'm not sure the world will cope,
with this hatred inside.

WINTER'S FIRE

As wind blows over a cold winter's fire
tracing the flames from wire to wire
hedging and growths on mountainous leaves
eating the turnips and straightening their weaves.

DIVERGING THROUGH THE DECADENCE

Diverging through the decadence of diverse
procedural deaths
underneath the undergrowths, there's a line
I do protest
signalling advances with remittance for the crest
nebulous enhancements, pounding heartbeats
in the chest.

FREEDOMS

An abundance of corruption
no end to its tale
you can cause a disruption
but will most likely fail
so enjoy all the freedoms that we've come to cherish
let your goodness shine and leave the evil to perish.

INCANDESCENT WITH RAGE

Incandescent with rage, I'd be a fool to engage
leave the puppets to run the stage
won't interrupt, just rattle their cage.

AN ILLUSTRIOUS HEDGEHOG

The moon was shining
the stars were burning bright
the leaves were lying
surrounded by the light
the birds were singing
it's the end of the night
as our thoughts lay restless
concerned by their plight
but then an illustrious hedgehog fell to the floor
laughing and joking like never before
a penguin sneezed only to rise again
led by the chicken, let's go back to the den.

THE ANSWER TO IT ALL

So many solutions but which one's right,
no longer the answer to constrain the light
I see it, I see it from all sides,
where there's one voice, there's many who abide
The answer, the answer to it all,
of that I'm uncertain, I cannot call.

SUPERSTITIOUS

I'm superstitious
why can't you see?
If I count to one
I've got to count to three
If I touch my sock
I've got to touch my shoe
when I look to the heavens
I get the flu
touching the table won't suffice
if I see a door, I have to turn twice.

FOREVER IN A BUBBLE

Forever in a bubble
a constant rainy cloud
wanting to feel emotion
failing to make a sound.

SANCTITY'S AMISS

Sanctity's amiss in this morning bliss
no time to reminisce
whilst these feelings persist
the cavities say it all
I am perspiring
kick it some more
'cause this cat's for hiring
this cat's for hiring?
Yes I'm not retiring
just aspiring, to see
a striking falsetto, with a rich harmony.

ISOLATION

Mr Isolation in isolation mode
tired of doing, doing what he's told
needs a new direction
to not be scared to fall
reach out for the stars
enlighten my soul
this ground's lost all control
I'm flying out of habit
spinning this round ball
feeding carrots to the rabbit
just make my dreams come true
sick of this path I'm taking
can't risk air turning blue
I don't want to be mistaken.

FEELINGS

I don't feel I deserve to have my say
one man's present is another man's prey
I care so much but I don't know why
because others wouldn't care if I were to die
you can dislike me intensely
I'll still wish you the best
remaining positive I will pass this test.

EXTOLLING THE REVERENCE

Extolling the reverence in congruous time
of Fortfield's stature, assessed and refined
all scarpered cognizance,
irreputable haze
mending with treason
the dulcet remains.

ENCOURAGEMENT

Get yourself out there
stop moping around
else your head will touch the floor
before you hit the ground
optimistic, you've got to stay
in a world where the greedy
eat their prey.

SENSELESS CONCLUSIONS

Try to explain but they don't understand
do your best
they get the upper hand
you can see it in their eyes
deluded to the skies
but they'll never realize
or even try to compromise.

Sick of the staring
the look of hate
the lack of compassion
I just can't relate.

The stupid comments
lack of thought
no common sense
it can't be taught.

Infuriating to talk to
refuse to listen
argue that black is white
they have no vision.

Everything's opposite to what it should be
we're living in a world where the people can't see.

The writings have all passed
and the rules have changed
and the thoughts in my head have rearranged.

Senseless conclusions take their toll
but you've just got to rise above it all.

Got to break free from this senseless reality,
got to be what I want to be.
Stop looking over my shoulder
before it's too late
because I'm getting older.

IF THE GOOD COME TOGETHER

Sophisticated charms,
causing alarm
renegades of silence
encouraged to disarm
effortlessly waiting,
prevaricating over pastures new
with lightning striking many,
unable to construe
but what can you do,
when the powers have blocked all roads
feeling entrenched, failing to decode?
Well, you must come back
you must never give in
as unpleasant as they are,
you cannot let them win
and although your cries of freedom
will likely fall on icy ground
if the good come together,
we could really change things round.

DISINGENUOUS

No acceptance to the friend's request,
it tore a little hole in my heart
but it's not something I'll regret,
we're obviously better off apart
I just don't get why they show interest,
then leave you high and dry.
Is it just because they know they can
and leave you wondering why?

A FORTUITOUS MESS

A fortuitous mess of anxiety
trembling amongst the shivers
I tried, but it was all in vain
I've sunk in many rivers.

WAITING

Waiting for love to swing my way
it doesn't matter what they say
it's hard to find decent,
to find caring
I don't want liars, I don't want daring
oh this is getting ever so wearing
I called Aunt Martha but they're overbearing.
"It will arrive one day," she said.
"Just you wait."
"Been doing that for years, Aunty, and still no date."
"Well, keep the faith and it will come
you will find happiness, a lifelong chum."

SKY

You got me feeling
when I should be reeling
so high in the sky
there ain't no ceiling.

LOVE

The first time I've fallen in love
in many, many years
do I shroud myself in doubt
or do I wipe away the tears?
You talk about fears ejecting
the heart from my soul
all I know is this feeling I have
is out of control
encapturing a darkness
lightening a seed
I could thank you forever
but the rain falls on me.

ALTERNATE REALITY

Alternate reality
twisted profanity
a dialogue of negligence
changing your sanity.

THERE'S NO RESTART

Yeah we've all got problems but the best thing to do
is to forget all the rubbish that has happened to you
yeah I know it sounds easy, I know it's hard
but you've got to look forward because there's no restart.

MOVING ON

Finding a way to move along
it won't be easy and it can't be wrong
they've taken enough energy from me
now it's time for me to be free
I can't believe how stupid I was
it was all because
I gave them the benefit of the doubt
I thought their love was something
I just couldn't live without
but really they had no compassion
and showed no remorse
and only thought of themselves during the course.

COLD

I like you but you are raging
don't think you appreciate our engagement
sanctimony's high, telling us why
we can't help get this over the line
I just want to know you
all that you do
say the word
you've got nothing to lose
go for a walk
drink some wine
take a flight
make you mine
breathe in the air
chill by the sea
not making the most of what this could be
you see life passes in an instant
so why waste time being distant?
All these days wondering why
will all be pointless when we die.
But I think you've chosen the route you're taking
full of lies and lots of faking
I know I'm not mistaken
a clear mind has overtaken
and although I am shaking
this heart is not for breaking.

MANIPULATION

You like to manipulate,
play games to stimulate
tell them one thing and me another
the truth is out there to discover
I need someone who I can trust
being pretty just ain't good enough.

HEY, DARLING

Hey, darling, I've got something to say to you
yes, darling, we can make a love that's true
no, darling, we still haven't talked that much
no, darling, you're a bit frosty, where's your human touch?

NO NEED FOR HATE

Flagellate, devastate
feel no need to procreate this hate
an invaluable state
free to debate
prolonged engagements can stimulate
to initiate peace, when you wish to abate
I'll no longer wait
breaking this door, to seal my fate.

WHAT HAPPENED TO THOSE TIMES OF ROMANCE?

Where did morals, where did they go?
I keep asking myself why they've fallen so low
what happened to the ballroom and those times of romance?
What happened to giving true love a chance?

CONSPICUOUS SOUNDS

In an internal lust of compulsion,
incurring divulsion
wayward passing of the tides
battles will commence, a serenade full of pride
conspicuous sounds of a merry-go-round
conspiring, conflating, my foot's underground
the smugness derives from their everlasting glow
unwilling to comprise of the feelings we can show.

ATTRACTION

Ain't no satisfaction
in this mystery of attraction.

ANTI-BULLIES

Not sure what the point is, if it's endless ridicule
they claim to be anti-bullies but think mocking
is really cool
they can dismiss the claimant's virtues
and town crier for the speech
upon discovering the sermon's values
they'll only talk when they preach
they'll use you as an inspiration source
no credit given, emotionally divorced
stealing your words, ideas without a mention
acquiring lots of cash, removing all attention.

CASUISTRY AT LIGHT

Casuistry at light
a chink in the armour of an illustrious knight
salubrious, divulged fright
a feeling unnecessary but feels so right.

TIRELESS EMOTION

A tireless emotion
of copious devotion
a single shot can come spare
an inevitable erosion,
of a depleted notion
hair in the fibre will tear.

PROPHETIC PROFUSION

Ain't no mystical illusion to prophetic profusion.

EMOTIONALLY DETACHED

The silence has broken
the lambs have awoken
and now they're spreading
the lies
for they've taken their token
cut loose their emotion
they do what they need to get by.

MULTIFARIOUS CONJECTURES

From a crest of a wave
to an imperial grave lost at sea
with no one to save, no one to
save but me
merchants of freedom,
tyrants of Rome
miscellaneous hearts,
I have no home
melancholy, the floor beds
unearth the steady flow
when will they learn?
Ever learn to grow
multifarious conjectures,
unwittingly narcotic
on Faldom Commons
there lies a neurotic.

STATURE

I don't have the stature to face the rapture
this will capture, the indubitable disaster
of advocating, in telling the master.

APATHY

Much acquiescence in society
so obsequious, it's sad to see
a propensity towards apathy
they prefer the persiflage and perfidy.

LACK OF THOUGHT

Accumulative frequencies of
imperative lack of thought
subjugating matters with
reasoning which can't be taught
whilst a walk on the wild side
might quell the underlay
bereft of forgiveness
one will only stray.

RAINCLOUDS

Catching rainclouds on your face
trying to dial, but there's no trace.

NO POINT IN DEBATING

Loquacious, esoteric, whining like a cleric
indeterminate, internecine, sapient, saccharine,
demarcating, attenuating, vituperative, ululating,
idiosyncratic, complicating, no point in debating.

SPIRITUAL

Spiritual reputation
forming powers of retribution
stealing solemnization
in aisles of dissolution
remainders of collation
no longer a solution
in controlling this plight
an elation in ablution.

RECLUSION

An incantation of obliteration
no justification for an abomination
reclusion ain't the solution
a spiritual high leads to devolution.

SEVERING MY SOUL

Severing my soul,
taking back control,
relieving these demons
which placed me in this hole
memories cannot fall,
conquer fear of time
savouring only scolds,
mercurial silenced minds.

SHINING SUN

You won't catch me whining when the sun is shining
lay your head back 'cause this deckchair's reclining
blue sky, time to fly
wave to the haters as I pass them by
you're so beautiful, you're so sweet
my love for you just can't compete
fell from heaven, her smile's a crime
a cut above, mighty fine
you see, our eyes met from a distance
her rosy cheeks, red lips
in a trial of persistence, I was longing for her kiss
it's been hours since she left me
no chance to say goodbye
and now the time has passed
I just want to cry and cry.

SOLACE

To surpass the paradigm
we bring solace to the crime
romanticize the framework
recalcitrant roads become sublime.

MASS POLLUTION

Obligatory solutions to the problem of
mass pollution
I hold no insight
on the grounds of this constitution.

FLOATING

Floating on pictorial pains of charisma
hedging out kites,
cutting through stigma
feelings only linger into negative signs
you're a cold creed of conscience stuck within time
barbaric manuals,
epicentres aportioned
refining enzymes,
lacking distortion.

FALLING

You see me falling
I see you fading away
you think I'm stalling
no I am here to stay.

ACT LIKE I MEAN NOTHING

Are you just like them?
You want to pretend
act like I mean nothing
like you're happy it's the end
well I don't believe you
I know it's not true
I think that you're worried what we have
will turn blue
but how do you know
if you don't even try?
We haven't talked enough
to warrant a goodbye.

BRIDLED WITH JOY

Eloquent diversities lay bound and besieged,
hobbling along, extreme pain in their knees
Holy besmirched but bridled with joy,
nevertheless, no gift to deploy.

STIGMA

So hard these days for one to obtain
always brushed aside, the stigma to blame
so much lack of opportunity, such little gain
a lifetime endorsement of neglect and pain
to look in those eyes and not want to change
you must be cold-hearted or even deranged.

SHALLOW WORLD

Where now to go in a world so shallow
a line can alter in a crumbling road
targets to aim with a sparkling arrow
tails will turn in this humble abode.

BLAND

Everything's so bland
it's been said before
please nod on command
mainstream media isolating the airwaves
answer on Wikipedia
this boredom will save me
let's all say the same thing
have a different opinion?
Then let your thoughts ring
nothing new,
nothing exciting
recreate this message
need some emotion in writing.

STULTIFYING

Chastising, romanticizing, advertising, bluebird rising,
enterprising, stigmatizing, stultifying, communizing.

DYING DREAMS

Everyone's back at work
everyone's back at school
no more dreams, they're dying
no more dreams for you
the end of your freedom
fun and games endured
now back to the grind
mind-numbing I'm assured.

NO APPRECIATION

Just fly me away to a new destination
I want to feel the love, the appreciation.

ACCUSATIONS

I fervently deny that accusation
will not be held at the hands of manipulation
for this salubrious path I chose
cannot be exposed
no head is half empty
in this humble abode.

CONTRADICTIONS

"Be real," they shout under their pretentious pout
contradicting themselves, all the way throughout
tell you to express opinions but when you do
you're too opinionated, it mustn't be true.
"Respect others," they cry but they don't respect them
belittling, every chance, admiring their gem
spending time criticizing, not truly happy
and whatever good you do, they'll refuse to see.

AMBITIONS

I have ambitions but they're getting me nowhere
I cry for dawn until dusk appears
I need sun but I have no sun chair
so for all the puppies, let's have three cheers.

NEPOTISM

Are your family rich?
Do you have friends we know?
If not, we don't care
we won't help you to grow
yes you have talent but nepotism is here to stay
so please say hello, repeat what your friends say.

ENCUMBERING

I will encumber the unwanted greens of a land
that's never seen
harbour the valiant lamp posts
with no light but lasting beams.

SUNSHINE ON THE HORIZON

I'm going to remain hopeful,
sunshine is on the horizon
there are better times ahead
I'm going to remain hopeful,
sunshine is on the horizon
that it'll reach me before I'm dead
because I am hopeful I will be content
as contented as one can be
I will have achieved some goals which my
memory will uphold
and inner peace will inhabit me.

SALUBRIOUS

His actions were salutary,
salubrious in fact
for a man who was once pernicious
his probity is now intact.

BRING ME ELATION

No time for stagnation
need some positive vibration
could you be the one to bring me elation?
No, I ain't got time for that, chucky,
no, I ain't got time for that, boo,
I'm entertaining the public 'cause this is what I do
so when they all come calling,
I'll be driving to see Billy Ray
I am the master, holy ground is where I lay.

UNINSPIRING

I must say, you are equally uninspiring
and inept at rhetorical questioning
thus foresight proceeding through
concepts of persuasion
in fact missing the point
and not engaging.

ENCOURAGE AND SUPPORT

Use the platform to encourage and support
less negative scowls, abiding retorts
ending in noughts
they're under your spell
here lies a great mind, you need to propel.

SUBSTANCE

Is there any stubble in the bubble?
Is there any wine in the crowd?
Is there any air perfusing
or shouting out loud?

SERENADING HOPELESS TREASURES

Masquerading faultless measures
undeterred from what lies beneath
serenading hopeless treasures in a
sanctuary of disbelief
ambuscading lifetime leisures
seeking light-hearted relief
we say hello to pleasures
and kiss goodbye to grief.

IN NEED OF FUN

Too much info flooding my brain
one more word, I'll go insane
need some fun, a little romance
to numb this pain, free me from this stance.

RHYTHMLESS PASSION

A ceiling, a lighting, a standing remain
a rhythmless passion that's become quite inane
insidious, egregious, sumptuous disdain,
elusive, obstreperous, released from this chain.

WORK

Work, work, work
and then you die
before you know it,
life's passed you by
the future looked bright
but now it looks dead
no time to map out
this feeling in your head
a penny for your sweat
a dime for your tears
they'll run you to the ground
then drown you with fears
there must be a better life to create
with less time wasted under the state
where we have less worries,
less chores,
less monotonous bores,
we'll eradicate more boundaries
and change all the laws.

DESPOTISM

Obsessed by celebrity
how false can one world be?
Respect their idols more than their family
brainwashed by the media
believe everything they're fed
no desire to question
a future to only dread
it's a catastrophe
whatever happened to humanity?
There's a better world for us to see
yeah, there's a better world for us to see
the truth is I'll be gone
at the summit of 'What went wrong'
many stains seeking removal
I no longer need your approval
their sycophantic game
I'm not one to pass the blame
I could never group up to ridicule
it's going too far, much too cruel.